What Is
EXERCISE SCIENCE?

Rebecca Woodbury, Ph.D., M.Ed.

Gravitas Publications Inc.

What Is
Exercise Science?

Illustrations: Janet Moneymaker

What Is Exercise Science? (hardcover)
ISBN 978-1-953542-66-3

Published by Gravitas Publications Inc.
www.gravitaspublications.com
www.realscience4kids.com

RS4K

Photo credits: Cover and Title Page, By Africa Studio, AdobeStock; Above, By bottomlayercz0 from Pixabaychild; P. 3. By amorn, AdobeStock; P. 5. By grafikplusfoto, AdobeStock; P. 7. By Rudy and Peter Skitterians from Pixabay; P. 13. By Africa Studio, AdobeStock P. 16. By Дмитрий Бурматов, AdobeStock; P. 17. By fermiart from Pixabay; P. 19. By Jihan, AdobeStock; P. 20. By Ermolaev Alexandr, AdobeStock; P. 21. By Robert Kneschke, AdobeStock

How does my body

jump a rope?

Like this!

How does my body run a race?

How does my body know
how to climb a tree?

How can I feed my body so I can lift heavy things?

Give it cheese?

All of these questions
are studied by exercise
science.

Exercise science explores...

...how the body works,

...how exercise changes the body,

...how the body uses food.

Exercise scientists want to find out the best way to ride a bike...

...the best way to feed a swimmer...

...the best way to hike a mountain...

Exercise science can help us...

Ooof!

...grow strong...

...stay healthy...

...win races.

How to say science words

exercise   (EK-suhr-siyz)

healthy   (HEL-thee)

muscle   (MUH-suhl)

science   (SIY-ens)

scientist   (SIY-en-tist)

www.ingramcontent.com/pod-product-compliance
Lightning Source LLC
Chambersburg PA
CBHW062333150426

42813CB00078B/2763